Candy

Kelly

Refresher

Greta

Refresher

Penny

Holly

Flip

Jay

Index

MERRY

KIM HARGREAVES

YARN

Rowan Big Wool

	XS	S	M	L	XL	
To fit bust	81	86	91	97	102	cm
	32	34	36	38	40	in
	3	3	4	4	5	x 100gm

(photographed in Heaven 004)

NEEDLES

1 pair 15mm (US 19) needles
1 pair 9mm (no 00) (US 13) needles

TENSION

7½ sts and 10 rows to 10 cm measured over stocking stitch using 15mm (US 19) needles.

BACK

Cast on 28 (30: 32: 34: 36) sts using 15mm (US 19) needles.
Beg with a K row, work in st st, shaping side seams by dec 1 st at each end of 5th and foll 4th row. 24 (26: 28: 30: 32) sts.
Work 3 (5: 5: 5: 5) rows, ending with a WS row.
Inc 1 st at each end of next and every foll 6th row until there are 30 (32: 34: 36: 38) sts.
Cont straight until back measures 29 (30: 30: 31: 31) cm, ending with a WS row.

Shape armholes

Cast off 2 sts at beg of next 2 rows.
26 (28: 30: 32: 34) sts.
Next row (RS) (dec): K2, K2tog, K to last 4 sts, K2tog tbl, K1, pick up loop lying between needles and place this loop on right needle (note: this loop does NOT count as a st), slip last st knitwise.
Next row (dec): P tog the first st and the loop, P1, P2tog tbl, P to last 4 sts, P2tog, P1, pick up loop lying between needles and place on right needle (note: this loop does NOT count as a st), slip last st knitwise. 22 (24: 26: 28: 30) sts.
Medium, large and extra large sizes only
Next row (RS) (dec): K tog tbl first st and the loop. K1, K2tog, K to last 4 sts, K2tog tbl, K1, pick up loop lying between needles and place this loop on right needle, slip last st knitwise.
- (-: 24: 26: 28) sts.
Medium and large sizes only
Next row: P tog the first st and the loop, P to last st, pick up loop lying between needles and place on right needle, slip last st knitwise.
Extra large size only
Next row (dec): P tog the first st and the loop, P1, P2tog tbl, P to last 4 sts, P2tog, P1, pick up loop lying between needles and place on right needle (note: this loop does NOT count as a st), slip last st knitwise. - (-: -: -: 26) sts.
All sizes
Next row (RS): K tog tbl first st and the loop, K to last st, pick up loop lying between needles and place this loop on right needle, slip last st knitwise.
Next row: P tog the first st and the loop, P to last st, pick up loop lying between needles and place on right needle, slip last st knitwise.
These 2 rows set the sts - armhole edge slip st selvedge and rem sts in st st.
Cont as set until armhole measures 20 (20: 21: 21: 22) cm, ending with a WS row.

Shape shoulders and back neck

Next row (RS): Cast off 2 (3: 3: 3: 3) sts, K until there are 5 sts on right needle and turn, leaving rem sts on a holder.
Work each side of neck separately.
Cast off 2 sts at beg of next row.
Cast off rem 3 sts.
With RS facing, rejoin yarn to rem sts, cast off centre 8 (8: 8: 10: 10) sts, patt to end.
Work to match first side, reversing shapings.

FRONT

Work as given for back until 6 rows less have been worked to start of shoulder shaping, ending with a WS row.

Shape neck

Next row (RS): Patt 8 (9: 9: 9: 9) sts and turn, leaving rem sts on a holder.
Work each side of neck separately.
Keeping armhole edge sts correct, dec 1 st at neck edge on next 2 rows, then on foll alt row.
5 (6: 6: 6: 6) sts.
Work 1 row, ending with a WS row.

Shape shoulder

Cast off 2 (3: 3: 3: 3) sts at beg of next row.
Work 1 row.
Cast off rem 3 sts.
With RS facing, rejoin yarn to rem sts, cast off centre 6 (6: 6: 8: 8) sts, patt to end.
Work to match first side, reversing shapings.

MAKING UP

PRESS all pieces as described on the information page.
Join right shoulder seam using back stitch, or mattress stitch if preferred.

Neckband

With RS facing and 9mm (US 13) needles, pick up and knit 9 sts down left side of neck, 6 (6: 6: 8: 8) sts from front, 9 sts up right side of neck, then 16 (16: 16: 18: 18) sts from back.
40 (40: 40: 44: 44) sts.
Beg with a **purl** row, work in st st for 4 rows.
Cast off **firmly** purlwise.
See information page for finishing instructions.

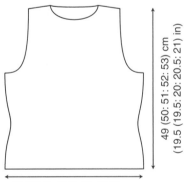

49 (50: 51: 52: 53) cm
(19.5 (19.5: 20: 20.5: 21) in)

40 (42.5: 45.5: 48: 50.5) cm
(15.5 (16.5: 18: 19: 20) in)

PENNY

KIM HARGREAVES

YARN

Rowan Biggy Print

	XS	S	M	L	XL	
To fit bust	81	86	91	97	102	cm
	32	34	36	38	40	in
	8	8	9	9	10	x 100gm

(photographed in 243)

NEEDLES

1 pair 20mm (US 36) needles

TENSION

5½ sts and 7 rows to 10 cm measured over stocking stitch using 20mm (US 36) needles.

BACK

Cast on 22 (24: 26: 28: 30) sts using 20mm (US 36) needles.

Beg with a K row, work in st st, shaping side seams by inc 1 st at each end of 5th (7th: 7th: 7th: 7th) and foll 6th row.
26 (28: 30: 32: 34) sts.

Cont straight until back measures 25 (26: 26: 27: 27) cm, ending with a WS row.

Shape armholes

Cast off 2 sts at beg of next 2 rows.
22 (24: 26: 28: 30) sts.

Dec 1 st at each end of next and foll 0 (0: 1: 1: 2) alt rows. 20 (22: 22: 24: 24) sts.
Cont straight until armhole measures 20 (20: 21: 21: 22) cm, ending with a WS row.

Shape shoulders

Cast off 3 sts at beg of next 2 rows, then 3 (4: 4: 4: 4) sts at beg of foll 2 rows.
Cast off rem 8 (8: 8: 10: 10) sts.

LEFT FRONT

Cast on 11 (12: 13: 14: 15) sts using 20mm (US 36) needles.

Beg with a K row, work in st st, shaping side seam by inc 1 st at beg of 5th (7th: 7th: 7th: 7th) and foll 6th row. 13 (14: 15: 16: 17) sts.
Cont straight until left front matches back to beg of armhole shaping, ending with a WS row.

Shape armhole

Cast off 2 sts at beg of next row.
11 (12: 13: 14: 15) sts.

Work 1 row.

Dec 1 st at armhole edge of next and foll 0 (0: 1: 1: 2) alt rows. 10 (11: 11: 12: 12) sts.
Cont straight until 3 rows less have been worked than on back to start of shoulder shaping, ending with a RS row.

Shape neck

Cast off 2 (2: 2: 3: 3) sts at beg of next row.
8 (9: 9: 9: 9) sts.

Dec 1 st at neck edge of next 2 rows, ending with a WS row. 6 (7: 7: 7: 7) sts.

Shape shoulder

Cast off 3 sts at beg of next row.

Work 1 row.

Cast off rem 3 (4: 4: 4: 4) sts.

RIGHT FRONT

Cast on 11 (12: 13: 14: 15) sts using 20mm (US 36) needles.

Beg with a K row, work in st st, shaping side seams by inc 1 st at end of 5th (7th: 7th: 7th: 7th) and foll 6th row. 13 (14: 15: 16: 17) sts.
Complete to match left front, reversing shapings.

SLEEVES (both alike)

Cast on 14 (14: 14: 16: 16) sts using 20mm (US 36) needles.

Beg with a K row, work in st st, shaping sides by inc 1 st at each end of 9th (9th: 3rd: 9th: 3rd) and every foll 8th row until there are 20 (20: 22: 22: 24) sts.

Cont straight until sleeve measures 43 (43: 44: 44: 44) cm, ending with a WS row.

Shape top

Cast off 2 sts at beg of next 2 rows.
16 (16: 18: 18: 20) sts.

Dec 1 st at each end of next and foll 2 (2: 1: 1: 2) alt rows, then on foll 3 (3: 5: 5: 5) rows.
Cast off rem 4 sts.

MAKING UP

PRESS all pieces as described on the information page.

Join shoulder seams using back stitch, or mattress stitch if preferred.

See information page for finishing instructions, setting in sleeves using the set-in method.

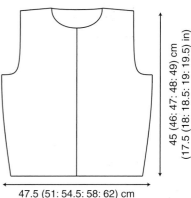

47.5 (51: 54.5: 58: 62) cm
(18.5 (20: 21.5: 23: 24.5) in)

45 (46: 47: 48: 49) cm
(17.5 (18: 18.5: 19: 19.5) in)

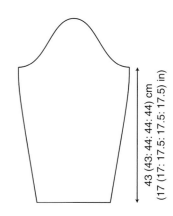

43 (43: 44: 44: 44) cm
(17 (17: 17.5: 17.5: 17.5) in)

GRETA

KIM HARGREAVES

YARN
Rowan Big Wool

	XS	S	M	L	XL	
To fit bust	81	86	91	97	102	cm
	32	34	36	38	40	in
A Merry Berry 006	4	4	5	5	6	x 100gm
B White Hot 001	2	2	2	3	3	x 100gm

NEEDLES
1 pair 15mm (US 19) needles

TENSION
7½ sts and 10 rows to 10 cm measured over stocking stitch using 15mm (US 19) needles.

BACK
Cast on 27 (29: 31: 33: 35) sts using 15mm (US 19) needles and yarn A.
Row 1 (RS): K0 (0: 0: 0: 1), P0 (1: 2: 3: 3), ★K2, P3, rep from ★ to last 2 (3: 4: 0: 1) sts, K2 (2: 2: 0: 1), P0 (1: 2: 0: 0).
Row 2: P0 (0: 0: 0: 1), K0 (1: 2: 3: 3), ★P2, K3, rep from ★ to last 2 (3: 4: 0: 1) sts, P2 (2: 2: 0: 1), K0 (1: 2: 0: 0).
Rep last 2 rows 3 times more, ending with a WS row.
Beg with a K row, work in st st, shaping side

seams by inc 1 st at each end of 3rd and foll 4th row, then on foll 6th row. 33 (35: 37: 39: 41) sts.
Work 1 row, ending with a WS row.
Using the **fairisle** technique described on the information page, starting and ending rows as indicated, cont in patt foll chart for body, which is worked entirely in st st, as folls:
Work 4 rows, ending with a WS row.
Shape raglan armholes
Keeping chart correct, cast off 2 sts at beg of next 2 rows. 29 (31: 33: 35: 37) sts.
Dec 1 st at each end of next and foll 4th row, then on every foll alt row until 11 (13: 13: 15: 15) sts rem.
Work 1 row, ending with a WS row.
Break yarn and leave sts on a holder.

FRONT
Work as given for back until 17 (19: 19: 21: 21) sts rem in raglan shaping.
Work 1 row, ending with a WS row.
Shape neck
Next row (RS): K2tog, K3 and turn, leaving rem sts on a holder.
Work each side of neck separately.
Next row: P2tog, P2.
Next row: K2tog, K1.
Next row: P2tog and fasten off.
With RS facing, slip centre 7 (9: 9: 11: 11) sts onto a holder, rejoin yarn to rem sts, K to last 2 sts, K2tog.
Work to match first side, reversing shapings.

SLEEVES
Cast on 19 (19: 19: 21: 21) sts using 15mm (US 19) needles and yarn A.
Row 1 (RS): P1 (1: 1: 2: 2), ★K2, P3, rep from ★ to last 3 (3: 3: 4: 4) sts, K2, P1 (1: 1: 2: 2).
Row 2: K1 (1: 1: 2: 2), ★P2, K3, rep from ★ to last 3 (3: 3: 4: 4) sts, P2, K1 (1: 1: 2: 2).
Rep last 2 rows 3 times more, ending with a WS row.
Beg with a K row, work in st st, shaping sides by inc 1 st at each end of 3rd (3rd: next: 3rd: next) and every foll 10th (10th: 8th: 10th: 8th) row until there are 27 (27: 29: 29: 31) sts.
Work 1 row, ending with a WS row.
Using the **fairisle** technique described on the information page, starting and ending rows as indicated, cont in patt foll chart for sleeve, which is worked entirely in st st, as folls:
Work 4 rows, ending with a WS row.

Shape raglan
Keeping chart correct, cast off 2 sts at beg of next 2 rows. 23 (23: 25: 25: 27) sts.
Dec 1 st at each end of next and foll 4th row, then on every foll alt row until 7 sts rem.
Work 1 row, ending with a WS row.
Left sleeve only
Next row (RS): K2tog, K2, cast off rem 3 sts. 3 sts.
Rejoin yarn with WS facing.

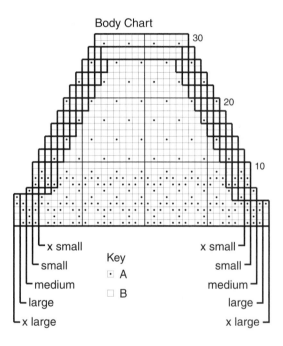

Body Chart

Key
⊡ A
☐ B

x small
small
medium
large
x large

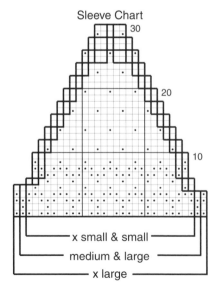

Sleeve Chart

x small & small
medium & large
x large

Right sleeve only
Cast off 3 sts at beg and dec 1 st at end of next row. 3 sts.
Both sleeves
Next row (WS): P3.
Cast off rem 3 sts.

MAKING UP
PRESS all pieces as described on the information page.
Join both front and right back raglan seams using back stitch, or mattress stitch if preferred.
Neckband
With RS facing, 15mm (US 19) needles and yarn B, pick up and knit 6 (6: 6: 7: 7) sts from left sleeve, 4 sts down left side of neck, knit across 7 (9: 9: 11: 11) sts from front holder, pick up and knit 4 sts up right side of neck, and 5 (6: 6: 6: 6) sts from right sleeve, then knit across 11 (13: 13: 15: 15) sts from back holder. 37 (42: 42: 47: 47) sts.
Row 1 (WS): K3, *P3, K2, rep from * to last 4 sts, P3, K1.
Row 2: P1, *K3, P2, rep from * to last st, P1.
Rep these 2 rows 5 times more.
Cast off **very loosely** in rib.
See information page for finishing instructions.

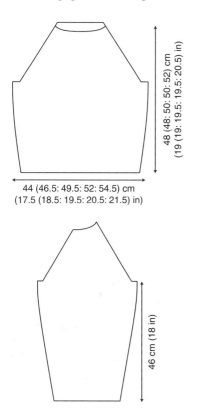

48 (48: 50: 50: 52) cm
(19 (19: 19.5: 19.5: 20.5) in)

44 (46.5: 49.5: 52: 54.5) cm
(17.5 (18.5: 19.5: 20.5: 21.5) in)

46 cm (18 in)

CANDY

KIM HARGREAVES

YARN
Rowan Big Wool
3   x   100gm
(photographed in Smitten Kitten 003)

NEEDLES
1 pair 9mm (no 00) (US 13) needles

TRIMMINGS
Piece of lining fabric 40 cm by 90 cm (15½ in by 35½ in)
Same size piece of iron-on interfacing (optional)
90 cm of 5 cm wide petersham ribbon

TENSION
10½ sts and 13 rows to 10 cm measured over stocking stitch using 9mm (US 13) needles.

FINISHED SIZE
Completed bag is approx 24 cm (9½ in) wide, 30 cm (12 in) tall and 10 cm (4 in) deep.

SIDES (make 2)
Cast on 6 sts using 9mm (US 13) needles.
Break yarn and set to one side for gusset.
Cast on 25 sts using 9mm (US 13) needles.
Work in garter st for 9 rows, ending with a RS row.

Shape for gussets
Next row (WS): Cast on and P 6 sts, K25, then P across gusset sts set to one side. 37 sts.
Next row (RS): K6, slip next st purlwise (for gusset fold line), K to last 7 sts, slip next st purlwise (for gusset fold line), K6.
Next row: Purl.
Rep last 2 rows 17 times more, and then first of these 2 rows again, ending with a RS row.
Work in garter st for 2 rows, ending with a RS row.
Cast off knitwise (on WS).

HANDLES (make 2)
Cast on 11 sts using 9mm (US 13) needles.
Work in garter st until handle measures 40 cm.
Cast off.

MAKING UP
PRESS all pieces as described on the information page.
If desired, from iron-on interfacing, cut 2 pieces same size as knitted side panels, trimming away 2 cm at upper edge, and apply interfacing to WS of knitted sections.
From lining fabric, cut 2 pieces same size as knitted side panels, adding seam allowance along all edges.
Join knitted side panels along cast-on edges (base) and row end edges (sides). Fold bag so that base/side seams meet and row end edges of garter st base match cast-on edges of side gussets, and sew seams.
Cut petersham ribbon into two equal lengths and wrap knitted handles around each strip. Slip stitch row end edges of handles together to enclose petersham, positioning seam centrally along strip. Positioning handles approx 8 cm apart, sew ends of handles in position inside upper edge of sides of bag.
Make up lining in same way as main knitted sections and slip lining inside bag. Turn under raw edge around top of bag and slip stitch lining in place.

Sal

KIM HARGREAVES

YARN
Rowan Big Wool

	XS	S	M	L	XL	
To fit bust	81	86	91	97	102	cm
	32	34	36	38	40	in
	5	5	6	6	7	x 100gm

(photographed in White Hot 001)

NEEDLES
1 pair 15mm (US 19) needles

ZIP
51 cm open-ended zip

TENSION
7½ sts and 10 rows to 10 cm measured over stocking stitch using 15mm (US 19) needles.

BACK
Cast on 27 (29: 31: 33: 35) sts using 15mm (US 19) needles.
Row 1 (RS): K0 (0: 0: 0: 1), P0 (1: 2: 3: 3), ★K2, P3, rep from ★ to last 2 (3: 4: 0: 1) sts, K2 (2: 2: 0: 1), P0 (1: 2: 0: 0).
Row 2: P0 (0: 0: 0: 1), K0 (1: 2: 3: 3), ★P2, K3, rep from ★ to last 2 (3: 4: 0: 1) sts, P2 (2: 2: 0: 1), K0 (1: 2: 0: 0).

Rep last 2 rows 3 times more, ending with a WS row.
Beg with a K row, work in st st, shaping side seams by inc 1 st at each end of 3rd and foll 4th row, then on foll 6th row. 33 (35: 37: 39: 41) sts.
Cont straight until back measures 26 cm, ending with a WS row.
Shape raglan armholes
Cast off 2 sts at beg of next 2 rows.
29 (31: 33: 35: 37) sts.
Dec 1 st at each end of next and every foll alt row until 9 (11: 11: 13: 13) sts rem.
Work 1 row, ending with a WS row.
Cast off.

LEFT FRONT
Cast on 14 (15: 16: 17: 18) sts using 15mm (US 19) needles.
Row 1 (RS): K0 (0: 0: 0: 1), P0 (1: 2: 3: 3), ★K2, P3, rep from ★ to last 4 sts, K2, P2.
Row 2: K2, ★P2, K3, rep from ★ to last 2 (3: 4: 0: 1) sts, P2 (2: 2: 0: 1), K0 (1: 2: 0: 0).
Rep last 2 rows 3 times more, ending with a WS row.
Beg with a K row, work in st st, shaping side seam by inc 1 st at beg of 3rd and foll 4th row, then on foll 6th row. 17 (18: 19: 20: 21) sts.
Cont straight until left front matches back to beg of raglan armhole shaping, ending with a WS row.
Shape raglan armhole
Cast off 2 sts at beg of next row.
15 (16: 17: 18: 19) sts.
Work 1 row.
Dec 1 st at armhole edge of next and every foll alt row until 9 (10: 10: 11: 11) sts rem, ending with a RS row.
Shape neck
Cast off 2 (3: 3: 4: 4) sts at beg of next row. 7 sts.
Dec 1 st at neck edge of next 3 rows **and at same time** dec 1 st at raglan edge on next and foll alt row. 2 sts.
Work 1 row.
Next row (RS): K2tog.
Next row: P1 and fasten off.

RIGHT FRONT
Cast on 14 (15: 16: 17: 18) sts using 15mm (US 19) needles.
Row 1 (RS): P2, ★K2, P3, rep from ★ to last 2 (3: 4: 0: 1) sts, K2 (2: 2: 0: 1), P0 (1: 2: 0: 0).

Row 2: P0 (0: 0: 0: 1), K0 (1: 2: 3: 3), ★P2, K3, rep from ★ to last 4 sts, P2, K2.
Rep last 2 rows 3 times more, ending with a WS row.
Beg with a K row, work in st st, shaping side seam by inc 1 st at end of 3rd and foll 4th row, then on foll 6th row.
17 (18: 19: 20: 21) sts.
Work to match left front, reversing shapings.

SLEEVES
Cast on 19 (19: 19: 21: 21) sts using 15mm (US 19) needles.
Row 1 (RS): P1 (1: 1: 2: 2), ★K2, P3, rep from ★ to last 3 (3: 3: 4: 4) sts, K2, P1 (1: 1: 2: 2).
Row 2: K1 (1: 1: 2: 2), ★P2, K3, rep from ★ to last 3 (3: 3: 4: 4) sts, P2, K1 (1: 1: 2: 2).
Rep last 2 rows 3 times more, ending with a WS row.
Beg with a K row, work in st st, shaping sides by inc 1 st at each end of 3rd and every foll 10th (10th: 8th: 10th: 8th) row until there are 27 (27: 29: 29: 31) sts.
Cont straight until sleeve measures 46 (46: 47: 47: 47) cm, ending with a WS row.
Shape raglan
Cast off 2 sts at beg of next 2 rows.
23 (23: 25: 25: 27) sts.
Dec 1 st at each end of next and every foll alt row until 5 sts rem.
Work 1 row, ending with a WS row.
Left sleeve only
Next row (RS): K2tog, K1, cast off rem 2 sts.
2 sts.
Rejoin yarn with WS facing.
Right sleeve only
Cast off 2 sts at beg and dec 1 st at end of next row. 2 sts.
Both sleeves
Next row (WS): P2.
Cast off rem 2 sts.

MAKING UP
PRESS all pieces as described on the information page.
Join raglan seams using back stitch, or mattress stitch if preferred.
Collar
With RS facing and 15mm (US 19) needles, pick up and knit 8 (9: 9: 10: 10) sts up right side of neck, 4 sts from right sleeve, 7 (10: 10: 13: 13) sts

from back, 4 sts from left sleeve, then 8 (9: 9: 10: 10) sts down left side of neck.
31 (36: 36: 41: 41) sts.
Row 1 (WS): K2, ★P2, K3, rep from ★ to last 4 sts, P2, K2.
Row 2: P2, ★K2, P3, rep from ★ to last 4 sts, K2, P2.
Rep these 2 rows until collar measures 20 cm, ending with a WS row.
Cast off **very loosely** in rib.
Insert zip into front opening, positioning top of zip 10 cm above neck pick-up row. Fold collar in half onto inside and stitch in position.
See information page for finishing instructions.

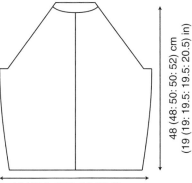

44 (46.5: 49.5: 52: 54.5) cm
(17.5 (18.5: 19.5: 20.5: 21.5) in)

48 (48: 50: 50: 52) cm
(19 (19: 19.5: 19.5: 20.5) in)

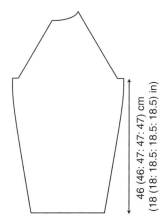

46 (46: 47: 47: 47) cm
(18 (18: 18.5: 18.5: 18.5) in)

JAY

KIM HARGREAVES

YARN
Rowan Biggy Print

	XS	S	M	L	XL	
To fit bust	81	86	91	97	102	cm
	32	34	36	38	40	in
	5	5	6	7	8	x 100gm

(photographed in 241)

NEEDLES
1 pair 20mm (US 36) needles

TENSION
5½ sts and 7 rows to 10 cm measured over stocking stitch using 20mm (US 36) needles.

BACK and FRONT (both alike)
Cast on 22 (24: 26: 28: 30) sts using 20mm (US 36) needles.
Beg with a K row, work in st st for 2 (4: 4: 4: 4) rows, ending with a WS row.
Cont in st st, shaping side seams by dec 1 st at each end of next and foll alt row. 18 (20: 22: 24: 26) sts.
Work 3 rows, ending with a WS row.
Inc 1 st at each end of next and every foll 4th row until there are 24 (26: 28: 30: 32) sts.
Cont straight until work measures 30 (31: 31: 32: 32) cm, ending with a WS row.

Shape armholes
Cast off 2 sts at beg of next 2 rows.
20 (22: 24: 26: 28) sts.
Dec 1 st at each end of next and foll 0 (0: 1: 1: 2) alt rows. 18 (20: 20: 22: 22) sts.
Cont straight until armhole measures 18 (18: 19: 19: 20) cm, ending with a WS row.
Shape shoulders
Cast off 2 sts at beg of next 4 rows.
10 (12: 12: 14: 14) sts.
Break yarn and leave sts on a holder.

MAKING UP
PRESS all pieces as described on the information page.
Join right shoulder seam using back stitch, or mattress stitch if preferred.
Neckband
With RS facing and 20mm (US 36) needles, knit 10 (12: 12: 14: 14) sts from front, then 10 (12: 12: 14: 14) sts from back. 20 (24: 24: 28: 28) sts.
Beg with a **purl** row, work in st st for 3 rows, ending with a WS row.
Cast off **very loosely**.
See information page for finishing instructions.

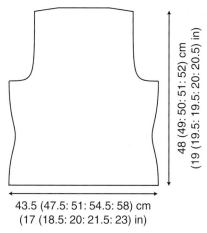

43.5 (47.5: 51: 54.5: 58) cm
(17 (18.5: 20: 21.5: 23) in)

48 (49: 50: 51: 52) cm
(19 (19.5: 19.5: 20: 20.5) in)

KELLY

KIM HARGREAVES

YARN
Rowan Biggy Print

	XS	S	M	L	XL
To fit bust	81	86	91	97	102 cm
	32	34	36	38	40 in
	15	16	17	18	19 x 100gm

(photographed in 240)

NEEDLES
1 pair 20mm (US 36) needles

TENSION
5½ sts and 7 rows to 10 cm measured over stocking stitch using 20mm (US 36) needles.

BACK
Cast on 31 (33: 35: 37: 39) sts using 20mm (US 36) needles.
Beg with a K row, work in st st until back measures 45 (46: 46: 47: 47) cm, ending with a WS row.
Shape armholes
Cast off 4 sts at beg of next 2 rows.
23 (25: 27: 29: 31) sts.
Cont straight until armhole measures 25 (25: 26: 26: 27) cm, ending with a WS row.
Shape shoulders and back neck
Next row (RS): Cast off 3 (3: 4: 4: 4) sts, K

until there are 5 (6: 6: 6: 7) sts on right needle and turn, leaving rem sts on a holder.
Work each side of neck separately.
Cast off 2 sts at beg of next row.
Cast off rem 3 (4: 4: 4: 5) sts.
With RS facing, rejoin yarn to rem sts, cast off centre 7 (7: 7: 9: 9) sts, K to end.
Work to match first side, reversing shapings.

FRONT
Work as given for back until 4 rows less have been worked to start of shoulder shaping, ending with a WS row.
Shape neck
Next row (RS): K8 (9: 10: 10: 11) and turn, leaving rem sts on a holder.
Work each side of neck separately.
Dec 1 st at neck edge on next 2 rows.
6 (7: 8: 8: 9) sts.
Work 1 row, ending with a WS row.
Shape shoulder
Cast off 3 (3: 4: 4: 4) sts at beg of next row.
Work 1 row.
Cast off rem 3 (4: 4: 4: 5) sts.
With RS facing, rejoin yarn to rem sts, cast off centre 7 (7: 7: 9: 9) sts, K to end.
Work to match first side, reversing shapings.

SLEEVES (both alike)
Cast on 19 (21: 21: 23: 23) sts using 20mm (US 36) needles.
Beg with a K row, work in st st, shaping sides by inc 1 st at each end of 7th and every foll 6th row to 23 (29: 27: 33: 29) sts, then on every foll 4th (4th: 4th: –: 4th) row until there are 31 (31: 33: –: 35) sts.
Cont straight until sleeve measures 53 (53: 54: 54: 54) cm, ending with a WS row.
Cast off **very loosely**.

MAKING UP
PRESS all pieces as described on the information page.
Join right shoulder seam using back stitch, or mattress stitch if preferred.
Collar
With RS facing and 20mm (US 36) needles, pick up and knit 7 sts down left side of neck, 7 (7: 7: 9: 9) sts from front, 7 sts up right side of neck, then 11 (11: 11: 13: 13) sts from back.
32 (32: 32: 36: 36) sts.

Beg with a **purl** row, work in st st until collar measures 25 cm, ending with a WS row.
Cast off **very loosely**.
See information page for finishing instructions, setting in sleeves using the square set-in method.

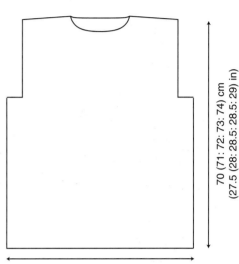

56.5 (60: 63.5: 67.5: 71) cm
(22 (23.5: 25: 26.5: 28) in)

70 (71: 72: 73: 74) cm
(27.5 (28: 28.5: 28.5: 29) in)

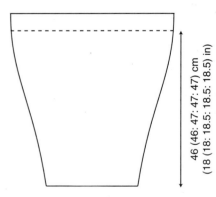

46 (46: 47: 47: 47) cm
(18 (18: 18.5: 18.5: 18.5) in)

DESIGN NUMBER 8

SMARTY

KIM HARGREAVES

YARN

Rowan Big Wool

A	Sherbet Lime	002	1 x	100gm
B	Smitten Kitten	003	1 x	100gm

NEEDLES

1 pair 9mm (no 00) (US 13) needles
1 pair 15mm (US 19) needles

TENSION

7½ sts and 10 rows to 10 cm measured over stocking stitch using 15mm (US 19) needles.

FINISHED SIZE

Hat measures approx 49 cm (19½ in) around head.

HAT

Cast on 42 sts using 9mm (US 13) needles and yarn A.
Row 1 (RS): K2, ★P2, K2, rep from ★ to end.
Row 2: P2, ★K2, P2, rep from ★ to end.
Rep these 2 rows 7 times more.
Row 17 (RS) (dec): (K2, P2, K2tog, P2) 5 times, K2. 37 sts.
Break off yarn A and join in yarn B.
Change to 15mm (US 19) needles.
Beg with a **purl** row, work in st st as folls:

Work 13 rows, ending with a WS row.
Shape crown
Row 1 (RS) (dec): (K4, K2tog) 6 times, K1. 31 sts.
Row 2: Purl.
Row 3 (dec): (K3, K2tog) 6 times, K1. 25 sts.
Row 4: Purl.
Row 5 (dec): (K2, K2tog) 6 times, K1. 19 sts.
Row 6 (dec): P1, (P2tog, P1) 6 times. 13 sts.

DESIGN NUMBER 9

NELLY

KIM HARGREAVES

YARN

Rowan Big Wool

A	Smitten Kitten	003	1 x	100gm
B	White Hot	001	1 x	100gm

NEEDLES

1 pair 15mm (US 19) needles
Large crochet hook

TENSION

7½ sts and 10 rows to 10 cm measured over stocking stitch using 15mm (US 19) needles.

FINISHED SIZE

Hat measures approx 49 cm (19½ in) around head.

Row 7 (dec): (K2tog) 6 times, K1. 7 sts.
Break yarn and thread through rem 7 sts. Pull up tight and fasten off securely.

MAKING UP

PRESS as described on the information page.
Join back seam, reversing seam for turn-back.
Using yarn A, embroider loops at top of crown as in photograph.

HAT

Cast on 7 sts using 15mm (US 19) needles and yarn A.
Row 1 (WS): P7.
Row 2: (K1, M1) 6 times, K1. 13 sts.
Row 3: P1, (M1P, P2) 6 times. 19 sts.
Row 4: (K3, M1) 6 times, K1. 25 sts.
Row 5: Purl.
Row 6: (K4, M1) 6 times, K1. 31 sts.
Row 7: Purl.
Row 8: (K5, M1) 6 times, K1. 37 sts.
Row 9: Purl.
Join in yarn B and beg with a K row, work in st st as folls:
Using yarn B work 2 rows.
Using yarn A work 2 rows.
These 4 rows form striped st st.
Work in striped st st for a further 7 rows, ending with a RS row.
Shape for earflaps and lower edge
Next row (WS): Cast off first 4 sts, P until there are 9 sts on right needle and slip these sts onto a holder for second earflap, cast off next 11 sts, P until there are 9 sts on right needle, cast off rem 4 sts.
Keeping striped st st correct, re-join appropriate yarn to last set of 9 sts with RS facing and cont as folls:
Work 1 row.
Dec 1 st at each end of next and every foll alt row until 1 st rem.
Slip this st onto crochet hook and work a chain of approx 28 cm before fastening off.
Complete second earflap to match first.

MAKING UP

PRESS as described on the information page.
Join back seam.

FAITH

KIM HARGREAVES

YARN
Rowan Big Wool

	XS	S	M	L	XL	
To fit bust	81	86	91	97	102	cm
	32	34	36	38	40	in
		1	1	1	2	2	x 100gm

(photographed in Sherbet Lime 002)

NEEDLES
1 pair 15mm (US 19) needles
Large crochet hook (optional)

TENSION
7½ sts and 10 rows to 10 cm measured over stocking stitch using 15mm (US 19) needles.

TOP
Cast on 49 (51: 53: 55: 57) sts using 15mm (US 19) needles.
Row 1 (RS): K to last st, pick up loop lying between needles and place this loop on right needle (note: this loop does NOT count as a st), slip last st knitwise.
Row 2 (dec): P tog the first st and the loop, P1, P2tog tbl, P to last 4 sts, P2tog, P1, pick up loop lying between needles and place on right needle (note: this loop does NOT count as a st),

slip last st knitwise.
Row 3 (dec): K tog tbl first st and the loop, K1, K2tog, K to last 4 sts, K2tog tbl, K1, pick up loop lying between needles and place this loop on right needle, slip last st knitwise.
Row 4 (dec): As row 2.
Rep rows 3 and 4, 3 times more.
31 (33: 35: 37: 39) sts.
Row 11 (RS) (dec): K tog tbl first st and the loop, K1, K2tog, K to last 4 sts, K2tog tbl, K1, pick up loop lying between needles and place this loop on right needle, slip last st knitwise.
Row 12: P tog the first st and the loop, P to last st, pick up loop lying between needles and place on right needle, slip last st knitwise.
Rep rows 11 and 12, 8 (9: 9: 10: 10) times more.
13 (13: 15: 15: 17) sts.

Rep rows 3 and 4 once more.
Cast off rem 9 (9: 11: 11: 13) sts.

MAKING UP
PRESS as described on the information page.
Make and attach 40 cm long crochet or twisted cords to all 4 corners of knitted panel.

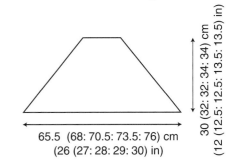

30 (32: 32: 34: 34) cm
(12 (12.5: 12.5: 13.5: 13.5) in)

65.5 (68: 70.5: 73.5: 76) cm
(26 (27: 28: 29: 30) in)

SNOWFLAKE

KIM HARGREAVES

YARN
Rowan Big Wool

A	White Hot	001	1	x	100gm
B	Smoky	007	1	x	100gm

NEEDLES
1 pair 15mm (US 19) needles
Large crochet hook

TENSION
7½ sts and 10 rows to 10 cm measured over stocking stitch using 15mm (US 19) needles.

FINISHED SIZE
Hat measures approx 49 cm (19½ in) around head.

HAT
Cast on 7 sts using 15mm (US 19) needles and yarn A.
Row 1 (WS): P7.
Row 2: (K1, M1) 6 times, K1. 13 sts.
Row 3: P1, (M1P, P2) 6 times. 19 sts.
Row 4: (K3, M1) 6 times, K1. 25 sts.
Row 5: Purl.
Row 6: (K4, M1) 6 times, K1. 31 sts.
Row 7: Purl.
Row 8: (K5, M1) 6 times, K1. 37 sts.
Row 9: Purl.
Using the **fairisle** technique described on the information page, work 8 rows in patt foll chart, which is worked entirely in st st, ending with a WS row.
Break off yarn A and cont using yarn B only.
Beg with a K row, work in st st for 4 rows, ending with a WS row.
Shape for earflaps and lower edge
Next row (RS): Cast off first 4 sts, K until there are 9 sts on right needle and slip these sts onto a holder for second earflap, cast off next 11 sts, K until there are 9 sts on right needle, cast off rem 4 sts.

Re-join yarn to last set of 9 sts with WS facing and cont as folls:
Work 1 row.
Dec 1 st at each end of next and every foll alt row until 1 st rem.
Slip this st onto crochet hook and work a chain of approx 28 cm before fastening off.
Complete second earflap to match first.

MAKING UP
PRESS as described on the information page.
Join back seam.

Key ■ A □ B

8

DESIGN NUMBER 12

JEWEL

KIM HARGREAVES

YARN
Rowan Biggy Print

	XS	S	M	L	XL	
To fit bust	81	86	91	97	102	cm
	32	34	36	38	40	in
	6	6	7	8	9	x 100gm

(photographed in 246)

NEEDLES
1 pair 20mm (US 36) needles

TENSION
5½ sts and 7 rows to 10 cm measured over reverse stocking stitch using 20mm (US 36) needles.

BACK
Cast on 22 (24: 26: 28: 30) sts using 20mm (US 36) needles.
Beg with a P row, work in rev st st for 2 (4: 4: 4: 4) rows, ending with a WS row.
Cont in rev st st, shaping side seams by dec 1 st at each end of next and foll alt row.
18 (20: 22: 24: 26) sts.
Work 3 rows, ending with a WS row.
Inc 1 st at each end of next and every foll 4th row until there are 24 (26: 28: 30: 32) sts.
Cont straight until back measures 30 (31: 31: 32: 32) cm, ending with a WS row.
Shape armholes
Cast off 2 sts at beg of next 2 rows.
20 (22: 24: 26: 28) sts.
Dec 1 st at each end of next and foll 0 (0: 1: 1: 2) alt rows. 18 (20: 20: 22: 22) sts.
Cont straight until armhole measures 18 (18: 19: 19: 20) cm, ending with a WS row.
Shape shoulders and back neck
Cast off 2 (3: 3: 3: 3) sts at beg of next row.
16 (17: 17: 19: 19) sts.
Next row (WS): Cast off 2 (3: 3: 3: 3) sts, K until there are 3 sts on right needle and turn, leaving rem sts on a holder.
Work each side of neck separately.
Work 1 row.
Cast off rem 3 sts.

With WS facing, rejoin yarn to rem sts, cast off centre 8 (8: 8: 10: 10) sts, K to end.
Cast off rem 3 sts.

FRONT
Work as given for back until 2 rows less have been worked to start of shoulder shaping, ending with a WS row.
Shape neck
Next row (RS): P7 (8: 8: 8: 8) and turn, leaving rem sts on a holder.
Work each side of neck separately.
Dec 1 st at neck edge on next row. 6 (7: 7: 7: 7) sts.
Shape shoulder
Cast off 2 (3: 3: 3: 3) sts at beg and dec 1 st at end of next row.
Work 1 row. Cast off rem 3 sts.
With RS facing, rejoin yarn to rem sts, cast off centre 4 (4: 4: 6: 6) sts, P to end.
Work to match first side, reversing shapings.

MAKING UP
PRESS all pieces as described on the information page.
Join right shoulder seam using back stitch, or mattress stitch if preferred.
Collar
With RS facing and 20mm (US 36) needles, pick up and knit 7 sts down left side of neck, 4 (4: 4: 6: 6) sts from front, 7 sts up right side of neck, then 9 (9: 9: 11: 11) sts from back.
27 (27: 27: 31: 31) sts.
Beg with a **knit** row, work in rev st st until collar measures 25 cm, ending with a WS row.
Cast off **very loosely**.
See information page for finishing instructions.

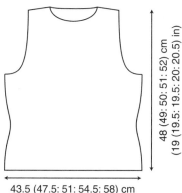

43.5 (47.5: 51: 54.5: 58) cm
(17 (18.5: 20: 21.5: 23) in)

48 (49: 50: 51: 52) cm
(19 (19.5: 19.5: 20: 20.5) in)

HOLLY

KIM HARGREAVES

YARN
Rowan Big Wool
    3   x   100gm
(photographed in Merry Berry 006)

NEEDLES
1 pair 15mm (US 19) needles

TENSION
7½ sts and 10 rows to 10 cm measured over stocking stitch using 15mm (US 19) needles.

FINISHED SIZE
Scarf is 25 cm (10 in) wide x 190 cm (75 in) long.

SCARF
Cast on 19 sts using 15mm (US 19) needles.
Work in garter st for 8 rows, ending with a WS row.
Patt as folls:
Row 1 (RS): Knit.
Row 2: K2, P15, K2.
Rows 3 to 12: As rows 1 and 2, 5 times.
Rows 13 to 18: Knit.
Rep last 18 rows 9 times more, ending with a WS row.
Work in garter st for a further 2 rows. Cast off.
See Pipin for making up instructions

LOTTIE

KIM HARGREAVES

YARN
Rowan Big Wool
A Heaven   004   1   x   100gm
B Smoky   007   1   x   100gm

NEEDLES
1 pair 15mm (US 19) needles

TENSION
7½ sts and 10 rows to 10 cm measured over stocking stitch using 15mm (US 19) needles.

FINISHED SIZE
Scarf is 20 cm (8 in) wide and 168 cm (66 in) long.

SCARF
Cast on 15 sts using 15mm (US 19) needles and yarn A.
Row 1 (RS): Using yarn A knit.
Row 2: Using yarn A K2, P11, K2.
Rows 3 to 14: As rows 1 and 2, 6 times.
Break off yarn A and join in yarn B.
Rows 15 to 28: As rows 1 and 2 but using yarn B.
Break off yarn B and join in yarn A.
Rep last 28 rows 5 times more, ending with 14 rows using yarn B. Cast off.
See Pipin for making up instructions

PIPIN

KIM HARGREAVES

YARN
Rowan Biggy Print
    5   x   100gm
(photographed in 248)

NEEDLES
1 pair 20mm (US 36) needles

TENSION
5½ sts and 8 rows to 10 cm measured over garter stitch using 20mm (US 36) needles.

FINISHED SIZE
Scarf is 22 cm (8½ in) wide x 205 cm (81 in) long.

SCARF
Cast on 12 sts using 20mm (US 36) needles.
Work in garter st until scarf measures 205 cm, ending with a WS row.
Cast off.

Holly, Lottie & Pipin
MAKING UP
PRESS as described on the information page.

REFRESHER

KIM HARGREAVES

YARN
Rowan Biggy Print
4   x   100gm
(photographed in 247)

NEEDLES
1 pair 20mm (US 36) needles

TENSION
5½ sts and 7 rows to 10 cm measured over
stocking stitch using 20mm (US 36) needles.

FINISHED SIZE
Scarf is 20 cm (8 in) wide x 205 cm (81 in) long.

SCARF
Cast on 11 sts using 20mm (US 36) needles.
Beg with a K row, work in st st until scarf measures
205 cm, ending with a WS row.
Cast off.

MAKING UP
PRESS as described on the information page.

FAB

KIM HARGREAVES

YARN
Rowan Big Wool
A Shriek   005   1   x   100gm
B Sherbet Lime 002   1   x   100gm

NEEDLES
1 pair 15mm (US 19) needles

TENSION
7½ sts and 10 rows to 10 cm measured over
stocking stitch using 15mm (US 19) needles.

FINISHED SIZE
Scarf is 18 cm (7 in) wide and 203 cm (80 in) long.

SCARF
Cast on 16 sts using 15mm (US 19) needles and
yarn A.
Row 1 (RS): Using yarn A knit.
Row 2: Using yarn A P into front and back of
first st, P to last 2 sts, P2tog.
Join in yarn B.
Row 3: Using yarn B knit.
Row 4: Using yarn B P into front and back of
first st, P to last 2 sts, P2tog.
These 4 rows form patt.

Continued overleaf

FLIP

KIM HARGREAVES

YARN
Rowan Biggy Print
2   x   100gm
(photographed in 246)

NEEDLES
1 pair 15mm (US 19) needles

TENSION
6 sts and 7 rows to 10 cm measured over
stocking stitch using 15mm (US 19) needles.

FINISHED SIZE
Hat measures approx 53 cm (21 in) around head.

HAT
Cast on 32 sts using 15mm (US 19) needles.
Beg with a K row, work in st st as folls:
Work 14 rows, ending with a WS row.
Shape crown
Row 1 (RS) (dec): (K2, K2tog) 8 times. 24 sts.
Row 2: Purl.
Row 3 (dec): (K1, K2tog) 8 times. 16 sts.
Row 4: Purl.
Row 5 (dec): (K2tog) 8 times. 8 sts.
Row 6: Purl.

Continued overleaf

LULU

KIM HARGREAVES

YARN
Rowan Big Wool
2 x 100gm
(photographed in Shriek 005)

NEEDLES
1 pair 9mm (no 00) (US 13) needles

TENSION
10½ sts and 13 rows to 10 cm measured over
stocking stitch using 9mm (US 13) needles.

FINISHED SIZE
Completed bag is approx 24 cm (9½ in) wide, 17
cm (6½ in) tall and 8 cm (3 in) deep.

SIDES (make 2)
Cast on 21 sts using 9mm (US 13) needles.
Row 1 (RS): Knit.
Row 2: P1, M1P, P to last st, M1P, P1.
Rep last 2 rows once more. 25 sts.
Beg with a K row, work in st st for 17 rows,
ending with a RS row.
Work in garter st for 2 rows.
Cast off knitwise (on WS).

FLAP
Cast on 23 sts using 9mm (US 13) needles.
Row 1 (RS): Knit.
Row 2: K2, P19, K2.
Rep last 2 rows 6 times more, ending with a WS
row.
Work in garter st for 3 rows.
Cast off knitwise (on WS).

GUSSET
Cast on 9 sts using 9mm (US 13) needles, and
knit 2 rows.
Beg with a **knit** row, work in st st until gusset
measures 55 cm, ending with a RS row.
Work in garter st for 2 rows.
Cast off knitwise (on WS).

STRAP
Cast on 5 sts using 9mm (US 13) needles.
Work in garter st until strap measures 50 cm.
Cast off.

MAKING UP
PRESS as described on the information page.
Sew one edge of gusset to side (row end) and
lower (cast-on) edge of one side panel, matching
ends of gusset to cast-off edges of side panel. Join
gusset to other side panel in same way. Position
cast-on edge of flap 3 cm down from upper
edge of one (back) side panel and stitch in place.
Fold flap over onto other (front) side panel. If
desired, sew a length of petersham ribbon to one
side of strap to prevent strap stretching. Make
pleats at top of gussets and sew ends of strap over
pleats.

Fab
Continued from previous page
Stranding yarn not in use loosely up side of
work, cont in patt until scarf measures approx
203 cm, ending after 2 rows using yarn A.
Cast off.

MAKING UP
PRESS as described on the information page.

Flip
Continued from previous page
Break yarn and thread through rem 8 sts. Pull up
tight and fasten off securely.

MAKING UP
PRESS as described on the information page.
Join back seam.

Photographer Joey Toller • Stylist Kim Hargreaves • Hair & Make-up Annabel Hobbs, Dottie Monaghan
Models Michelle Vacher, Nathalie Rich, Zhanna Begdullayeva, Chloe Hardy

INFORMATION PAGE

TENSION

Obtaining the correct tension is perhaps the single factor which can make the difference between a successful garment and a disastrous one. It controls both the shape and size of an article, so any variation, however slight, can distort the finished look of the garment.

We recommend that you knit a square in pattern and/or stocking stitch (depending on the pattern instructions) of perhaps 5 - 10 more stitches and 5 - 10 more rows than those given in the tension note. Press the finished square under a damp cloth and mark out the central 10cm square with pins. If you have too many stitches to 10cm try again using thicker needles, if you have too few stitches to 10cm try again using finer needles. Once you have achieved the correct tension your garment will be knitted to the measurements indicated in the size diagram shown at the end of the pattern.

SIZING AND SIZE DIAGRAM NOTE

The instructions are given for the smallest size. Where they vary, work the figures in brackets for the larger sizes. **One set of figures refers to all sizes**.

Included with every pattern in this magazine is a '**size diagram**', or sketch of the finished garment and its dimensions. The purpose of this is to enable you to accurately achieve a perfect fitting garment without the need for worry during knitting. The size diagram shows the finished width of the garment at the under-arm point, and it is this measurement that the knitter should choose first; a useful tip is to measure one of your own garments which is a comfortable fit. Having chosen a size based on width, look at the corresponding length for that size; if you are not happy with the total length which we recommend, adjust your own garment before beginning your armhole shaping - any adjustment after this point will mean that your sleeve will not fit into your garment easily - don't forget to take your adjustment into account if there is any side seam shaping. Finally, look at the sleeve length; the size diagram shows the finished sleeve measurement, taking into account any top-arm insertion length. Measure your body between the centre of your neck and your wrist, this measurement should correspond to half the garment width plus the sleeve length. Again, your sleeve length may be adjusted, but remember to take into consideration your sleeve increases if you do adjust the length - you must increase more frequently than the pattern states to shorten your sleeve, less frequently to lengthen it.

CHART NOTE

Someof the patterns in the book are worked from charts. Each square on a chart represents a stitch and each line of squares a row of knitting. Each colour used is given a different symbol or letter and these are shown in the **materials** section, or in the **key** alongside the chart of each pattern.

When working from the charts, read odd rows (K) from right to left and even rows (P) from left to right, unless otherwise stated.

KNITTING WITH COLOUR

There are two main methods of working colour into a knitted fabric: **Intarsia** and **Fairisle** techniques. The first method produces a single thickness of fabric and is usually used where a colour is only required in a particular area of a row and does not form a repeating pattern across the row, as in the fairisle technique.

Intarsia: Cut short lengths of yarn for each motif or block of colour used in a row. Joining in the various colours at the appropriate point on the row, link one colour to the next by twisting them around each other where they meet on the wrong side to avoid gaps.

Fairisle type knitting: When two or three colours are worked repeatedly across a row, strand the yarn **not** in use loosely behind the stitches being worked. It is advisable not to carry the stranded or "floating" yarns over more than three stitches at a time, but to weave them under and over the colour you are working. The "floating" yarns are therefore caught at the back of the work.

FINISHING INSTRUCTIONS

After working for hours knitting a garment, it seems a great pity that many garments are spoiled because such little care is taken in the pressing and finishing process. Follow the following tips for a truly professional-looking garment.

PRESSING

Darn in all ends neatly along the selvage edge or a colour join, as appropriate.

Block out each piece of knitting using pins and gently press each piece, omitting the ribs, using a warm iron over a damp cloth. **Tip**: Take special care to press the edges, as this will make sewing up both easier and neater.

STITCHING

When stitching the pieces together, remember to match areas of colour and texture very carefully where they meet.

Use a seam stitch such as back stitch or mattress stitch for all main knitting seams, and join all ribs and neckband with a flat seam unless otherwise stated.

CONSTRUCTION

Having completed the pattern instructions, join left shoulder and neckband seams as detailed above.

Sew the top of the sleeve to the body of the garment using the method detailed in the pattern, referring to the appropriate guide:

Square set-in sleeves: Set sleeve head into armhole, the straight sides at top of sleeve to form a neat right-angle to cast-off sts at armhole on back and front.

Set-in sleeves: Set in sleeve, easing sleeve head into armhole.

JOIN SIDE AND SLEEVE SEAMS.

Slip stitch pocket edgings and linings into place.

Sew on buttons to correspond with buttonholes. After sewing up, press seams and hems.

Ribbed welts and neckbands and any areas of garter stitch should not be pressed.

ABBREVIATIONS

K	knit	**rep**	repeat	**tbl**	through back of loop
P	purl	**alt**	alternate	**M1**	make one stitch by picking up
st(s)	stitch(es)	**cont**	continue		horizontal loop before next stitch
inc	increas(e)(ing)	**patt**	pattern		and knitting into back of it
dec	decreas(e)(ing)	**tog**	together	**yfwd**	yarn forward
st st	stocking stitch (1 row K, 1 row P)	**mm**	millimetres		
garter st	garter stitch (K every row)	**cm**	centimetres		
beg	begin(ning)	**in(s)**	inch(es)		
foll	following	**RS**	right side		
rem	remain(ing)	**WS**	wrong side		
rev	revers(e)(ing)	**sl1**	slip one stitch		
		psso	pass slipped stitch over		

EXPERIENCE RATINGS

= Easy, straight forward knitting

= Suitable for the average knitter

STOCKIST INFORMATION

ROWAN OVERSEAS DISTRIBUTORS

BELGIUM
Pavan
Koningin Astridlaan 78
B9000 Gent
Tel: (32) 9 221 8591

CANADA
Diamond Yarn
9697 St Laurent
Montreal
Quebec
H3L 2N1
Tel: (514) 388 6188
www.diamondyarns.com

Diamond Yarn (Toronto)
155 Martin Ross
Unit 3
Toronto
Ontario
M3J 2L9
Tel: (416) 736 6111
www.diamondyarns.com

DENMARK
Individual stockists
- please contact Rowan for details

FRANCE
Elle Tricot
8 Rue du Coq
67000 Strasbourg
Tel: (33) 3 88 23 03 13
www.elletricote.com

GERMANY
Wolle & Design
Wolfshovener Strasse 76
52428 Julich-Stetternich
Tel : (49) 2461 54735.
www.wolleundesign.de

HOLLAND
de Afstap
Oude Leliestraat 12
1015 AW Amsterdam
Tel : (31) 20 6231445

HONG KONG
East Unity Co Ltd
Room 902,
Block A
Kailey Industrial Centre
12 Fung Yip Street
Chai Wan
Tel : (852) 2869 7110.

ICELAND
Storkurinn
Kjorgardi
Laugavegi 59
Reykjavik
Tel: (354) 551 82 58

JAPAN
DiaKeito Co Ltd
2-3-11 Senba-Higashi
Minoh City
Osaka
Tel : (81) 727 27 6604
www.rowanintl-jp.com

NORWAY
Hera
Tennisun 3D
0777 OSLO
Tel: (47) 22 49 54 65

SWEDEN
Wincent
Norrtulsgaten 65
11345 Stockholm
Tel: (46) 8 673 70 60

U.S.A.
Rowan USA
5 Northern Boulevard
Amherst
New Hampshire 03031
Tel: (1 603) 886 5041/5043

For details of U.K. stockists or any other information concerning this book please contact:
Rowan Yarns, Green Lane Mill, Holmfirth, West Yorkshire HD9 2DX
Tel: +44 (0)1484 681881   Fax: +44 (0)1484 687920
Email: seasons@knitrowan.com www.knitrowan.com

Nelly

Lulu

Fab

Pipin

Merry

Faith

Lottie

Jewel

Snowflake